03/04

MOTHER TERESA

Protector of the Sick

by
Linda Carlson Johnson

A BLACKBIRCH PRESS BOOK

WOODBRIDGE, CONNECTICUT

Published by Blackbirch Press, Inc.
One Bradley Road, Suite 205
Woodbridge, CT 06525

©1991 Blackbirch Press, Inc.
First Edition

Manufactured in the United States of America

10 9 8 7 6 5 4 3 2 1

Library of Congress Cataloging-in-Publication Data

Johnson, Linda Carlson.
    Mother Teresa: protector of the sick / Linda Carlson Johnson.
    (The Library of famous women)
    Includes bibliographical references and index.
    Summary: A biography of a nun who founded the Missionaries of Charity to work with the destitute and dying, and was awarded the Nobel Peace Prize in 1979.
    ISBN 1-56711-034-7
    1. Teresa, Mother, 1910–   —Juvenile literature. 2. Nuns—India—Calcutta—History—Juvenile literature. 3. Missionaries of Charity—History—Juvenile literature. [1. Teresa, Mother, 1910–   2. Nuns. 3. Missionaries. 4. Missionaries of Charity.]
I. Title. II. Series.
BX4408.5.Z8J64 1990
271'.97—dc20
[B]   90-47213
[92]   CIP
                                                     AC

Contents

| | Introduction | A Place to Die | 5 |

Introduction 5

Chapter One — A Place to Die ... 6

Chapter Two — The Path to Calcutta ... 11

Chapter Three — The Nightmare City ... 16

Chapter Four — The Missionaries of Charity ... 23

Chapter Five — So Beautiful ... 29

Chapter Six — The Growing Work of Mother Teresa ... 38

Chapter Seven — Can You Help? ... 48

Chapter Eight — An Important Prize for the Saint of the Gutters ... 50

Chapter Nine — The Work Continues ... 53

Glossary—*Explaining New Words* ... 61

For Further Reading ... 62

Introduction

Mother Teresa is a famous woman. All over the world, people know the face of this tiny Catholic nun. In 1979, she won the Nobel Prize for Peace because of what she had done to help the poor and dying of the world. People have often called her "the saint of the gutters." But whenever people have asked Mother Teresa to talk about herself, she has refused, saying that her life is not important. "I am nothing," she has often said.

Instead of talking about herself, Mother Teresa has always talked about her work for God. This book is about that work.

(Opposite page) **Mother Teresa has always had a special relationship with children.**

Chapter 1

A Place to Die

Bulls are sacred in India. They roam the streets freely.

It is 1955. Crowds of people hurry to their jobs in the busy city of Calcutta, India. They don't seem to notice a woman lying on the pavement just outside the hospital. The woman is dying. She is so sick that she can't stop the rats from nibbling at her feet.

Then, a tiny woman wearing a blue-trimmed white sari stops and stands over the dying woman. The stranger wastes no time. Though she is only 4 feet, 11 inches tall and weighs less than 100 pounds herself, she picks the woman up and carries her inside the hospital, where she asks for help.

Hospital officials say that the dying woman can't stay because she has no money to pay for treatment. Even if the woman had the money, the hospital wouldn't take her, officials say. She has a disease that the other patients might catch.

The tiny woman, a Catholic nun named Mother Teresa, refuses to remove the dying woman from the hospital. Finally, hospital officials agree to take her as a patient.

Mother Teresa leaves the hospital, but she cannot get the woman out of her mind. She is one of the many poor people that Mother Teresa has found dying alone in the streets of Calcutta.

Then Mother Teresa has an idea. She goes to the city officials and asks if they will give her a place that she can make into a home for the dying. She says that the town will not have to give her any money or help, just a place.

India is a country with a very large population. This causes many problems such as overcrowding, starvation, and disease.

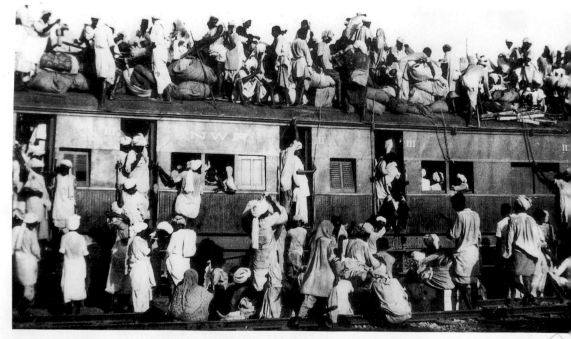

Mother Teresa and her nuns turned an abandoned building into a home for the dying, named Nirmal Hriday.

The city officials say Mother Teresa can use a building next to a Hindu temple. This place, once a shelter for Hindu pilgrims traveling to the temple, is now abandoned and run-down. Drunks, gamblers, and homeless people use it as a hang out. But Mother Teresa has a feeling that this is just the right place for her home for the dying. She knows that she will find many dying people near the shelter because Hindus who are dying often try to reach the temple.

Mother Teresa calls her new home for the dying Nirmal Hriday, which means the Place of the Pure Heart. She and the other nuns who work with her begin to walk the streets of Calcutta to find dying people to bring to Nirmal Hriday for help.

But some Hindu people near the temple don't trust Mother Teresa. These people think that she and the other nuns will try to get Hindu people to become Christians like her. People begin to threaten Mother Teresa's life. They stand outside Nirmal Hriday and shout at Mother Teresa and her nuns, telling them to go away. As the nuns walk the streets, people often throw stones at them.

The nuns refuse to leave, so a group of people call the police and complain about them. The police chief says he will go to Nirmal Hriday to see what is going on.

The police chief walks into the dimly lit hospital for the dying. He sees Mother Teresa bending over a dying woman, putting medicine on the woman's open sores, which are crawling with maggots. The police chief can hardly stand the stench coming from the dying woman. He spends some time watching the nuns as they tend other dying men and women in the two rooms of Nirmal Hriday. Then he tells the people waiting for his decision that he will be glad to kick Mother Teresa out of the building. But, he adds, "Before I do, you must get your mothers and sisters to do the work Mother Teresa is doing."

The crowd is silent. They have seen the people inside Nirmal Hriday. They know that no one in their families would do what Mother Teresa is doing. They give up on their idea of having her kicked out. But they don't stop throwing stones at her and the other nuns and shouting at them to leave.

Then, one day, Mother Teresa sees a crowd of people on the pavement outside Nirmal Hriday. She goes outside to see what is going on. The crowd is gathered around a man who is dying in his own vomit. No one will touch the man because he has a terrible disease, cholera, that is highly contagious.

Mother Teresa walks through the crowd to the man. She picks him up and takes him inside Nirmal Hriday, puts him in a bed, and washes him. The man soon dies in his clean bed, with Mother Teresa at his side.

After that day, the Hindus outside Nirmal Hriday stop giving Mother Teresa trouble. The man who died was a Hindu priest that everyone respected. Now the people respect Mother Teresa, this strange little Catholic nun who risked her own life just to give their priest a clean place to die.

Chapter 2

The Path to Calcutta

Mother Teresa came from a place far from India, a country that is now known as Yugoslavia. How did she find her way to the slums of Calcutta?

Before she became Mother Teresa, her name was Agnes Gonxha Bojaxhiu. Here, in 1928, she is 18 years old.

Mother Teresa was born in 1910 in a city called Skopje. Her parents gave her the name Agnes Gonxha Bojaxhiu. Her father was a grocer and her mother took care of the family, which included Agnes and her brother and sister.

Agnes went to a government school and belonged to a girls' group at the Catholic church called the Sodality of Mary.

At 12, Agnes first felt "the desire to belong completely to God," to become a nun. But from the time she was 12 until she was 18, she forgot about being a nun and just enjoyed growing up.

During this time, however, Agnes learned more about what it could mean to serve

God. Missionaries who had left Skopje to work in India sent home letters about their work there. Once, missionaries who had come home from India visited Skopje and described the work of some nuns in Calcutta called the Sisters of Loreto.

When Agnes was 18, she was in church one afternoon praying. Her heart began to sing and she felt full of joy. She heard a voice, which she knew was the voice of God, calling her to save Him and others.

Mother Teresa's birthplace, Skopje, in what is now Yugoslavia.

Agnes knew at that moment that she had to leave her happy home to become a missionary in India. She joined the Sisters of Loreto and traveled to Ireland to learn English. At that time, India was ruled by the British. Agnes was to teach British children in a school in India, so she had to learn to speak the children's language.

Later that year, 1929, Agnes was sent to school in Darjeeling, India, to teach the children of rich British tea plantation owners and wealthy Indians. It was here that Agnes took her first vows as a nun and changed her name to Mary Teresa. All of the nuns used "Mary" as their first name to honor Mary, the mother of Jesus. Agnes chose Teresa as her second name, the one she would be known by, because it belonged to her favorite saint, Saint Teresa. This Teresa had often been called "the little flower" and was known for serving God in small, humble ways.

In 1931, young Sister Teresa was sent to Calcutta to teach geography in another school run by the Sisters of Loreto, St. Mary's High School. The school was beautiful, with its white buildings, green lawns and gardens, and children in neatly pressed uniforms. Most of the students were daughters of middle-class people in Calcutta. But just outside the school's high walls were the *bustees*, or slums, of a section of Calcutta known as Moti Jhil. In the *bustees* of Moti Jhil, there were open sewers and mountains of stinking trash. Dirty children roamed the streets in search of food. Sick and starving people lay in the streets waiting to die.

The young nun took the name of Teresa, after her favorite saint.

Even though Sister Teresa was happy teaching at St. Mary's, she was touched by the suffering of the people of Moti Jhil. She asked permission to go out on Saturdays and after school to help the poor. She would collect a few supplies, such as leftover food, aspirin, and bandages, and walk the streets, helping the poor in whatever way she could.

In 1937, Sister Teresa took her final vows as a nun and continued to teach at St. Mary's. Nine years later, she traveled to Darjeeling for a retreat, a time for prayer with other nuns. On her way back to Calcutta on the train, Sister Teresa felt, for the second time, that she had received a clear message from God. This day, which many nuns now call the "Day of Inspiration," was September 10, 1946. Mother Teresa said later that what she felt that day was a "call within a call." God had first called her to go to India, and now she was being called to serve some special people. "The message was quite clear," she said. "I was to leave the convent and help the poor while living among them. It was an order."

But Sister Teresa had one problem. She had promised obedience to her order, the Sisters of Loreto. And she had been told by the Sisters of Loreto that she was to serve as a teacher inside the walls of St. Mary's. "I knew where I belonged," Mother Teresa would later say, "but I didn't know how to get there."

Sister Teresa went to her superiors and told them of her calling. She asked permission to live on the streets of Calcutta, serving the poor. The other nuns did not approve of Sister Teresa's plan. They thought of her as a rather ordinary nun who often forgot to do even small tasks, such as lighting candles, when she was supposed to. Besides, her superiors said, they could not make such a decision themselves. When a nun wanted to leave the convent, she had to have the permission of the Pope, head of the Catholic church.

Sister Teresa waited patiently as a year passed, then almost another. Finally, permission was granted by the Pope. Sister Teresa would become the Reverend Mother Teresa, head of her own order of nuns. This order would be called the "Missionaries of Charity" and would be dedicated to helping the poor. But for now, Mother Teresa would be alone.

To learn more about helping the sick of Calcutta, Mother Teresa first went to another place in India called Patna, for four months of medical training from American missionary nuns. Here, she learned such things as how to give shots, clean wounds, and apply bandages properly. Then she returned to the hot, dirty streets of Calcutta. At age 36, Mother Teresa left the convent for good.

Chapter 3

The Nightmare City

Teresa became a teacher with the Sisters of Loreto, in the early 1930s.

For Mother Teresa, leaving the convent was much more difficult than leaving her family had been. It was here that she had given her life in service to Jesus, here that she had received her training as a nun, here that she had been happy as a teacher of children. And she left the convent with almost nothing.

Mother Teresa had exchanged her black and white nun's habit for a cheap white cotton sari trimmed in blue. Only 4 feet, 11 inches tall, she looked very small and fragile wrapped in this traditional Indian dress. She had only five rupees (less than two dollars) in her pocket. She was as poor as the people she had vowed to serve.

Poor People Everywhere

Calcutta, once called the City of Palaces because of its beautiful buildings, had been known almost from its founding in 1690 as a city filled with poor people. Many of the people around Calcutta lived off the land, but there were often floods and famines. At these times, the rural people would come to the city in search of food and shelter, but they found little of either.

In the year that Mother Teresa left the convent, 1948, things in Calcutta were even worse than usual. The year before, India had won its independence from British rule. When this had happened, Bengal, the part of India where Calcutta was, had been divided. A new country called East Pakistan had been formed. But many of the people living in East Pakistan wanted to remain in India, so they flooded into the nearest city, Calcutta. Already overpopulated, Calcutta became choked with millions of poor people.

Some of the poor lived in earth huts with tile roofs. Others lived in makeshift tents made of tarpaper or cloth. Some lived without a roof on traffic islands or on sidewalks. None of the poor had water or electricity. When they could find food, they cooked it over open fires wherever they were living, so the air of the slums was always thick with smoke. There were no public bathrooms, so people had to use the

Calcutta:The Nightmare City

(At left)
The poor people of Calcutta live in the street. They have little food and no running water or electricity.

(Below)
When Mother Teresa first came to India, there were thousands of refugee children in the streets. They often were sick and starving. Many did not have parents to take care of them.

streets. Piles of garbage were everywhere because the city did not have enough trucks to cart it away. Cows, sacred to the Hindus, wandered the streets freely. There were not enough beds for the sick in the hospitals, so many sick people had to lie on the hospital floors. But these were the lucky ones. Many more sick people lay in the streets with no one to help them.

Middle-class and rich people as well as poor people lived in Calcutta. Most of these people were Hindus, who believe in a caste, or class, system. People born into a poor caste, Hindus believe, should stay in that caste. Other people who are more well-off should not try to help them. To many non-Hindus, the caste system seems cruel. But the Hindus also believe that people are reborn many times in many forms. They believe that a poor person who lives a good life may be reborn to a better life the next time.

On the streets of Calcutta, then, Hindus of higher castes could walk by the poor without trying to help. In fact, they would think it was wrong for them to help. Even those Hindus who didn't believe strictly in a caste system did little to help the poor, partly because there were so many and the situation seemed impossible.

So, the street scene in Calcutta was a strange one. Men and women in crisp, clean clothes hurried from air-conditioned apartments to their jobs. Yet outside these buildings, on the streets and sidewalks, was the other Calcutta, the home of the poor. Here, women picked lice from children's hair and people lay dying of starvation.

Beginning the Work

It was this Calcutta that Mother Teresa had vowed to serve. She began walking, searching for a place to live. She learned much about being poor, even on that first day. She confessed in her diary, "While looking for a home, I walked and walked until my arms and legs ached. I thought how much they [the poor] must ache in body and soul looking for a home, food, health."

Sometimes, she offered just a hug of comfort to someone who was dying.

Mother Teresa, though she was weak and unsure, knew she could not go back to the convent. She knocked on doors of shacks to ask how she could help. She begged for scraps of food and gave most of them away. She begged for medical supplies and began treating the sick on the street. Sometimes, she offered just a hug of comfort to someone who was dying.

One special problem Sister Teresa saw was that many poor children had no chance for an education. But, before she taught any lessons, she dunked the children in a tank of water and, using soap she had begged for, taught them how to wash themselves. Then she picked up a stick and began to draw letters in the earth because she had no blackboard and no books. More children came the next day, and more the next. The school kept growing, and people began to donate supplies.

Meanwhile, Mother Teresa had been given the gift of a home of her own. Father Henry, a Catholic priest who knew what Mother Teresa was doing, had been visiting the sick mother of a man named Michael Gomes. Father Henry asked Michael if he knew of a place Mother Teresa could stay. Michael's daughter reminded her father that their own house had an empty floor upstairs. Mother Teresa agreed to take one of the rooms on that floor. She brought with her a few empty boxes and crates, a chair, and a little suitcase containing her only other sari.

Mother Teresa's life's work had begun. Before long, she would not be doing her work alone.

Chapter 4

The Missionaries of Charity

One day not long after she had gone out on her own from the convent, Mother Teresa heard a knock on her door. When she opened it, she saw a 19-year-old Hindu girl named Subashini Das, a former student from St. Mary's.

"Mother, I have come to join you," the girl said.

"It will be a hard life. Are you prepared for it?" Mother Teresa replied.

Subashini said that she was prepared. As a new sister, she took a new name. She chose Agnes, in honor of Mother Teresa, and exchanged her expensive sari for a plain one just like Mother Teresa's. One month later, another new sister came. By 1950, 12 sisters had come, most of them former students of Mother Teresa from St. Mary's. Many of these girls were from

Mother Teresa is a physically small woman, only 4 feet 11 inches tall.

wealthy Hindu families, yet they willingly gave up their riches to serve the poor. Over the 40 years that Mother Teresa was head of the Missionaries of Charity, thousands of young women from all over the world joined the order to serve the poor.

Who Can Join?

In the beginning, Mother Teresa decided on four requirements for her Missionaries of Charity. Young women who wish to join must have healthy bodies and minds because the work they do is hard. They must have an ability to learn, even though no formal education is required. They must have common sense. And they must be cheerful because they will be serving Jesus, and Mother Teresa believed they could not do that with a long face.

For the first six months after a girl comes to Mother Teresa's order, she is called a "come and see." She lives and works with the sisters, but she is not a sister herself. At the end of the six months, she decides whether she will join. After about eight more years, if she still wants to be a sister, she takes her final vows and stays with the order for the rest of her life.

In Mother Teresa's order, new sisters take the same vows all other nuns take: poverty, chastity, and obedience. But each new sister in the Missionaries of Charity also takes a fourth vow of "whole-hearted free service to the poorest of the poor."

A Life of Poverty and Service

What is the life of a Sister of Charity like? The young women who come to serve give up everything they own. In return, they are given two cotton saris and some under-clothes; a tin bucket to wash them in; a plate and a cup; some prayer books; and pencil, pen, and paper. They never have any money, and they must never accept any gifts for themselves, not even food from their families, without permission. In the beginning, Mother Teresa wanted her sisters to eat only rice and salt, like the poor of Calcutta. But other sisters convinced her that the sisters needed to be fed well if they were to survive the hard work they would do among the sick and dying. So, the sisters eat simple foods such as flat bread, bananas, rice, vegetables, and some meat and fish.

All over the world, the sisters of the Missionaries of Charity follow the same schedule that Mother Teresa and her first group of sisters followed in 1950, when the order began. Six days a week, the sisters get up

...Each new sister...also takes a fourth vow of "whole-hearted free service to the poorest of the poor."

In order to control the spread of disease, the Sisters of Charity must scrub the floors of the hospital.

at 4:30 AM and prepare for prayer at 5 AM. At 6 AM, everyone attends mass, a church service. At 6:45 AM, some of the sisters go to breakfast while others wash one of their two saris in their tin buckets. Then the two groups switch places. At 7:50 AM, all the sisters gather for prayer, then they head out to their duties serving the poor. Some go to the home for the dying, others to feeding or medical stations, children's homes, schools, or homes for the sick. At 12:15 PM, all the sisters come back for lunch and prayers. They rest for half an hour, read and pray for another half an hour, then go back out to serve the poor. At 6:30 PM they return for Holy Hour, a time of singing and prayer. Supper is at

7:30 PM, followed by a half hour of recreation, which gives the sisters their first chance all day to talk to each other. At 9 PM, night prayers begin, and at 10 PM, the sisters sleep. All, that is, except Mother Teresa herself, who would often work late into the night, even when she became old and had a painful heart condition.

One day a week, the sisters have a day of reflection, rest, and prayer.

God in Disguise

In Calcutta, every young woman who arrived to serve in the Missionaries of Charity would quickly learn what the work of the order was all about. That first day, she would go to Nirmal Hriday, the home for the dying, to help in the work there. But before she left, Mother Teresa would tell the young woman to remember that when she touched the body of any sick or dying person, she would be touching the body of God in disguise. In the Bible it says that whoever feeds the hungry, clothes the naked, or helps the sick would be helping God.

Often, Mother Teresa would check on how her new "come and sees" were doing. One day, she watched a young woman caring for a dying man. He had maggots crawling out from open sores on his body, and his body stank. From an arm's-length distance, the young woman was using tweezers to remove the maggots one by one. Mother Teresa came over to the young woman to show her what she was doing wrong. Mother Teresa bent very close to the man's wounds. Using a razor, she gently scraped away the maggots and smiled at the man as she worked, despite the overwhelming odor. The young woman soon learned what Mother Teresa taught her that day—that the closer she came to the sick and dying in love, the closer she would come to God.

Mother Teresa explained that her sisters are not social workers, though they help the poor; not nurses or doctors, though they apply bandages and give shots; not teachers, though they teach. Instead, she said, her sisters serve God by helping the poor: "Our life has no other reason or motivation." The Missionaries of Charity, Mother Teresa often said, are in the business of doing "something beautiful for God."

Chapter 5

So Beautiful

A young, unwed mother cradles a small boy in her arms. The boy's legs are horribly deformed. Mother Teresa reaches out her hand to stroke the child's head. "So beautiful," she whis-pers, a smile on her face.

Mother Teresa always has time for the young people of the street.

A man walks up to Mother Teresa, presses some money into her hand, then walks away. "Isn't that beautiful?" Mother Teresa says to her companion.

Mother Teresa visits her home for abandoned children. At this home, there are newborn babies who have been rescued from trash heaps or left at the Mother House doorstep. Some babies are so small that they can barely move. Mother Teresa bends over one of the smallest babies. When she moves, Mother Teresa beams. "See, there's life in her!" she cries.

Mother Teresa also runs a home for abandoned children.

Amid sadness, pain, and suffering, Mother Teresa always found beauty—in a boy deformed yet loved by his mother, in a man who wanted to give money to the work of the sisters, in a baby with a chance for life.

Shantinagar, a Place of Beauty

One of the most beautiful places in India, Mother Teresa felt, was a place called Shantinagar, a Missionaries of Charity home for lepers. Leprosy is a disease that causes skin sores and can deaden nerve endings. If left untreated, leprosy can cause its victims to lose deadened parts of their bodies, such as their hands or feet. The disease thrives in warm countries such as India and is contagious, so lepers must be kept apart from other people while they are treated. In India, lepers have always been considered part of the lowest caste, called the "untouchables." These untouchables are the outcasts of Indian society. Even lepers' own families shun them. They are forced to beg and steal so they can survive.

At Shantinagar and other such homes throughout India, the lepers find help from the Missionaries of Charity. Many lepers are cured. For others, treatment stops the disease from becoming worse.

Mother Teresa brightens the day of a sick boy.

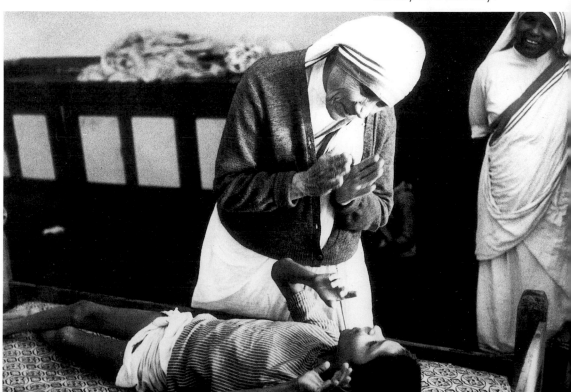

But even for the lepers who cannot be treated, there is comfort and a place to live and work. And there is beauty.

At Shantinagar, people with mutilated feet and hands learn to weave cloth to make bedsheets, bandages, towels, and clothing. Other lepers act as hospital helpers and gardeners. The grounds of Shantinagar are beautiful. Even inside the buildings there are flowers.

The most important thing the lepers find at Shantinagar is love. One Christmas, Mother Teresa came to Shantinagar to tell the lepers that the disease they had was not a sin and that they had a special gift—a God who loved them.

One leper, an old man so severely disfigured by his disease that he was hard to look at, came up to Mother Teresa and asked her to repeat what she had said. "I have always heard that nobody loves us," the man said. "It is wonderful to know that God loves us."

Beauty in Sacrifice

Mother Teresa found beauty in people that others saw as ugly or deformed because she saw that they were God's creatures. She also saw beauty in sacrifice. To

Lepers can become disfigured by their disease, often losing parts of limbs.

sacrifice means to give up something that is important.

Mother Teresa often told the story of a Hindu family that made a great sacrifice. Mother Teresa learned that this family with eight children was starving, so she brought them some rice. When Mother Teresa arrived, she saw that the children had the glazed look in their eyes that comes from starvation. Yet before the mother of the family prepared any of the rice for her own children, she took half of the rice next door to another starving family, which was Muslim. Often, Muslims and Hindus do not get along because they are of different faiths. When Mother Teresa asked the Hindu woman why she had given the rice away to this Muslim family, the woman said simply, "They are hungry also."

Mother Teresa remembered two other special sacrifices, one made by a man and one made by a small boy. The man, completely paralyzed except for his right arm, enjoyed one thing—smoking cigarettes. Yet, for one week, he did not smoke cigarettes and instead sent the money he would have spent to Mother Teresa.

The four-year-old boy knew of Mother Teresa's work among the poor and wanted

The most important thing the lepers find at Shantinagar is love.

to help, but he had no money to give. So he did not eat sugar for three days; instead, he brought the sugar to Mother Teresa so she could give it to those who had none.

Beauty in a Child

"Every child has been created for greater things, to love and to be loved, in the image of God," Mother Teresa once said.

Children have always been special to Mother Teresa. From the beginning of her work, she devoted time and effort to saving children. She started schools to educate the children of the slums, and she started homes for abandoned children.

In a poor city such as Calcutta, many babies are born to parents who cannot feed them, so the babies are left—on sidewalks, in trash cans, outside police stations, on the doorstep of the Missionaries of Charity Mother House. At all the city hospitals of Calcutta, officials know that if a mother leaves the hospital without her baby, the baby will find a home with the Sisters of Charity. Some of these babies weigh less than two pounds when they arrive.

The sisters, as well as doctors and nurses, care for the children. Some die. Many who survive are retarded, mentally ill, or

Mother Teresa, who has worked hard to create homes for orphans, once said, "Every child has been created for greater things...."

deformed, but they all receive the same love. And many are adopted by childless couples all over the world.

Each time she visited one of the homes for orphaned and abandoned children, Mother Teresa would be surrounded by little ones wanting her attention. Always, she would smile. Often she would say, "Aren't they beautiful?"

Beauty in Death

To Mother Teresa, there is beauty in all life. And, where there is love, there is beauty in death.

Mother Teresa told the story of a woman she once found in a dustbin. Her hair was matted, her body was covered with sores, and she was burning up with fever. She was crying, but not because of her physical pain. "My son did this to me," she sobbed.

Mother Teresa took the woman home and tried to convince the woman to forgive her son before she died. The woman finally did, but Mother Teresa never forgot that woman who felt so unwanted.

In the home for the dying, Nirmal Hriday, there is great pain and suffering. But the Missionaries of Charity make sure that no one feels unwanted or unloved.

"Each person, at the moment of receiving

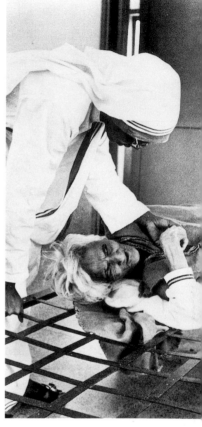

One of the sisters at Nirmal Hriday comforts an elderly dying woman.

my love, is the only person in the world," Mother Teresa said.

Not everyone who enters Nirmal Hriday dies. About half recover enough to leave. But everyone who enters Nirmal Hriday receives love and care. Mother Teresa taught the Missionaries of Charity to treat Hindus, Muslims, Christians, and even atheists (people who don't believe in any god) with the same love.

At Nirmal Hriday, there is a large room for men patients and a large room for women patients. The beds are plain, and the light inside the building is dim. The sisters and other helpers work among the sick quietly—washing them, feeding them, changing their bedclothes, cleaning their wounds, giving them medicine, holding their hands. Those closest to death are moved to the front of the room so that they can be watched and comforted.

Mother Teresa has taught her workers that love is the most important gift they can give the dying, or anyone else. She told the story of a woman, eaten alive by maggots and worms, who was brought to Nirmal Hriday. She lived only a short time, but for that time, Mother Teresa cared for her. Mother Teresa said she would never forget the smile on the woman's face and the words she spoke as she died: "Thank you."

Mother Teresa said that in her smile, the woman had given her much more than she could ever have given the woman.

Mother Teresa visits the patients of Nirmal Hriday.

Chapter 6

The Growing Work of Mother Teresa

Mother Teresa was awarded the first Pope John XXIII Peace Prize in 1971.

When Mother Teresa left the convent at St. Mary's in 1948, she was alone. By 1950, 12 sisters had joined her on the second floor of Michael Gomes's house in Calcutta, and the Pope had officially named Mother Teresa's group the Missionaries of Charity.

By 1952, Mother Teresa had started Nirmal Hriday, the home for the dying. And the Missionaries of Charity had found a new home, which is still their Mother House today. Mother Teresa had been looking for a house for her growing group of sisters, but had not had any luck. Her old friend, Father Henry, knew of a rich Muslim man who wanted to sell his house and land. Father Henry offered the man less than the price of the land, and the man accepted because he knew that Mother Teresa and her sisters would live and work in the house.

At first, Mother Teresa refused the house because she thought it was too big. There were three buildings on the property, and the main house was far too large for her group of sisters. But Father Henry convinced her to take the house. He told Mother Teresa that many more young women would be joining her. Mother Teresa finally agreed to move into the house that would be the home of the Missionaries of Charity for the rest of her life.

The Co-Workers of Mother Teresa

In 1954, a group called the Co-Workers of Mother Teresa began to help the sisters. This group began when Ann Blaikie, an English lawyer working in Calcutta, volunteered to buy toys for children at Christmas. Mother Teresa said toys would not be necessary, but clothing would be welcome. Ann Blaikie and her group bought clothing. Then, when the Muslim holiday of Ramadan came, Mother Teresa asked Ann if she would buy clothing again, this time for Muslim children. Then, Mother Teresa asked for clothing for Hindu children for their festival of Diwali. Once again, the Co-Workers came through.

Forty years later, the Co-Workers of Mother Teresa number more than 3 million, and they are from 70 countries. These Co-Workers are not nuns or priests. They are people of all faiths—Christians, Muslims, Hindus, and many others—who pray for the work of Mother Teresa and do what is needed to help the Missionaries of Charity. Sometimes that means collecting clothing for children, making bandages to use in centers for the sick, or raising money to buy medicine. Some Co-Workers travel to Calcutta to work side by side with the sisters. But often they work for the poor in their own communities. Mother Teresa has always told them to "practice charity first in the home, then among neighbors, then in their locality, in their country, and finally in the world."

⬥

"Practice charity first in the home, then among neighbors...and finally in the world."

From Calcutta to the World

Mother Teresa followed her own advice as her own work grew. In the early years, her work was only in Calcutta, where she and her sisters established many schools and centers for the sick, including lepers. Mother Teresa never set out to make her work grow; it just happened because she saw a need. Because there were lepers in Calcutta, for example, Mother Teresa wanted to serve them. She would set herself up near a sewage drain where lepers gathered, and she would begin to treat them and talk to them. Soon, more lepers would gather around Mother Teresa and her sisters.

There were so many lepers in Calcutta that Mother Teresa wanted to build medical stations, called dispensaries, all over the city. One city official objected because he didn't want a dispensary for the untouchables in his neighborhood. Instead of being angry at the man, Mother Teresa decided to have mobile dispensaries, trucks to carry medicine to lepers all over the city. She thanked the official for his objections because she said she never would have had the idea of mobile dispensaries without him. Now, she said, she could serve even more lepers!

News of Mother Teresa and her work began to spread. Soon, people were coming to Mother Teresa from all over the world to ask for help. When Mother Teresa saw that help was needed, she gave help. If a crippled man needed artificial legs that he could get only in another country, Mother Teresa would go to that country to ask officials to help. They almost always did.

When Mother Teresa heard that there were people suffering in another country,

Mother Teresa and the Missionaries of Charity perform work all over the world. Here, a visit to Manhattan in New York City is needed to help victims of AIDS and homelessness.

she would go there herself to see the situation. If she felt that the Missionaries of Charity should help, she would bring back five or six sisters to start a service to the poor in that country. By the early 1960s, there were new houses in Ceylon, Tanzania, Australia, Venezuela, and Italy. Though Mother Teresa had no plan for more growth, the work continued to expand. More houses were started—for famine victims in Africa, for rape victims in Pakistan, for AIDS victims and the homeless in New York City. By 1990, there were charity houses in more than 70 countries around the world.

In many of these places, the Missionaries of Charity are men as well as women. In 1963, a friend of Mother Teresa, an Australian priest named Brother Andrew who had worked for years in Calcutta, started a branch of the Missionaries of Charity for men. Wearing jeans, T-shirts, and silver crosses around their necks, the Brothers of Charity follow the same schedule and do the same work as the Sisters of Charity. The Brothers of Charity have run Shanti-nagar, the largest of the Missionaries of Charity homes for lepers in India, since 1974. By 1990, there were more than 400 Brothers of Charity laboring for the poor around the world.

Operating by Faith

From the first day Mother Teresa left the convent, she operated by faith. Though she only had five rupees to her name, Mother Teresa gave four of them away to the poor. When a Catholic priest asked for the last rupee she had, she hesitated for only a second before giving it to him, even though she did not know where any more money would come from. Several days later, the priest came back and gave Mother Teresa an envelope with 50 rupees in it. From that day on, Mother Teresa said, she knew God would bless her work.

In 1962, a sister called her from Agra, another city in India, to say that 50,000 rupees were needed for a children's home. Mother Teresa told the sister she did not have the money. A few minutes later, the phone rang again. A man told Mother Teresa she had won an award of money for her work in the Philippines. She asked the man how much money she would receive. He said about 50,000 rupees. Mother Teresa hung up the phone and said, "I guess God wants a children's home in Agra."

On another occasion, the Pope himself called Mother Teresa to ask her to start a branch of the Missionaries of Charity in Rome, even though there were thousands of nuns and priests already working there. Mother Teresa came to Rome to see what work needed to be done. She set herself up in the roughest, most dangerous part of the city. She and her sisters walked the crime-ridden streets unafraid. Mother Teresa even asked several teenagers known to be bullies to help her sisters set up a nursery so that single mothers in the area could work. The boys helped willingly.

Mother Teresa never worried about where the money or supplies would come from to do her work. Often, people simply sent money to her or dropped off gifts at the Mother House. Once, when the Pope visited Calcutta, he gave Mother Teresa his white Cadillac. She promptly auctioned it off for money, then used the money to set

Mother Teresa never worried about where the money or supplies would come from to do her work.

In May of 1983, Mother Teresa met with Pope John Paul II in Vatican City.

up one of the first of her many homes for lepers.

In 1970, when Mother Teresa was in London, a heroin addict died of an overdose at her feet. She told Ann Blaikie, who was now living in London, that the Co-Workers there should start a home for addicts. Mother Teresa found a house and offered the owner 6,000 pounds for it. The owner accepted the offer, even though it was 3,000 pounds less than she had been asking. The only trouble was, Mother Teresa had no money. So she made a trip around England to visit Co-Workers. She carried an old knitting bag with her. She did not ask for money, but when she returned to the Blaikie's house, she said to Ann and her husband John, "I think there is some money in my bag." John counted the money. It came to 5,995 pounds. Amazed, John added the last five pounds needed to buy the house.

Mother Teresa continued to work in Calcutta, but she was often called to help in other parts of India and all over the world. When she traveled by train, she rode in the cheapest cars, sometimes sleeping in the baggage racks. Traveling by plane was often difficult because it was so expensive. She once offered to work as a flight attendant so she could fly free. When the Prime Minister of India, Indira Gandhi, heard what had happened, she arranged with Air India airline for Mother Teresa to fly free—as a passenger—for the rest of her life. Mother Teresa gratefully accepted.

Mother Teresa always accepted offers of help, as long as they could be useful in her work with the poor. But she accepted little else.

On airplanes, she refused to accept the dinners that were offered to her. Instead, she put the food in her bag and would often ask the flight attendants if she could have the other passengers' leftovers to give the poor.

When Mother Teresa was awarded the Nobel Prize, she asked that the traditional banquet not be held in her honor. Instead, she asked for the money that would have been spent on the dinner so that she could use it to help the poor.

Once, when Mother Teresa began to work in South America, she was given a house full of expensive furniture and carpeting. She threw these things out, and even turned off the hot water. She didn't want the poor to think that her sisters were living better than they were.

In the Mother House in Calcutta, the sisters live without any luxuries. Even though the weather is extremely hot, there is only one fan. That fan is in the front room of the house, and it is turned on only when guests are visiting. Once, the sisters were offered a washing machine. They took a vote and decided not to accept the gift. They said they preferred to wash their own saris every day in their tin buckets.

Once, the sisters were offered a washing machine. They took a vote and decided not to accept the gift. They...preferred to wash their own saris...in their tin buckets.

Chapter 7

Can You Help?

People from all over the world travel to India to meet and work with Mother Teresa.

As Mother Teresa's work spread around the world, she became so famous that people often traveled to India just to meet her.

Mother Teresa always gave her autograph and allowed people to watch the work. But she often asked visitors, "Can you help?"

Courtney Tower, a writer who came to interview Mother Teresa and write a story about her work, ended up helping. In his story, he wrote that he learned how to sit with a dying man, holding his hand, letting him know he had a friend.

Another writer, Mark Jacobsen, came to Calcutta, just to get Mother Teresa's autograph. She asked him to help. Jacobsen didn't stay, but when he returned to his home in New York City, he noticed a homeless man begging outside his apartment building. He had given the man money before, but he had never thought about him as a person. He befriended the man and began doing things like taking him out to lunch. Suddenly, because Mark Jacobsen had met Mother Teresa, poverty was no longer something just to talk about.

Former governor of California Jerry Brown spent time working with Mother Teresa.

Jerry Brown, the former governor of California, went to Calcutta because he wanted to see what was so special about this woman, Mother Teresa. She put him to work right away at Nirmal Hriday. He bathed men and cleaned up after them when they soiled their beds. He fed the men and brought them water when they asked for it. He knelt close to dying men and held their hands. In three weeks, he saw 12 men die. He helped to wrap them in cotton sheets to be burned or buried, depending on their religious custom.

His experience at Nirmal Hriday left Jerry Brown a changed man. He said, "Mother Teresa challenges our whole way of life. She lives as if it were God himself lying there in the streets crying out for help. What does that mean for how we live each day? This is a question I can't get out of my mind today, back in America."

Chapter 8

An Important Prize for the Saint of the Gutters

Mother Teresa always makes time to see anyone who needs her.

Mother Teresa had won many awards in the more than 30 years she had worked among the poor. She had become known the world over as "the saint of the gutters." Yet, when the news reached her that she had won the 1979 Nobel Prize for Peace, she was shocked.

"I am unworthy," she said. The Nobel Prize is given each year to the one person or group in the world that has done the most in the cause of world peace. Mother Teresa did not think she deserved such an honor. She said there were many people far wiser and smarter than she was. She agreed, however, to accept the prize, not for herself, but "in the name of the poor." She flew to Stockholm, Sweden, for the award ceremony.

Hundreds of people, men in tuxedos and women in formal gowns, had gathered in

In 1979, Mother Teresa received the Nobel Peace Prize. She used the cash part of the award to start a new home for lepers.

the great hall to hear what the nun in the simple cotton sari and sandals would have to say. Many people were shocked by the Mother Teresa they saw. She looked much older than her 69 years. Her tiny body was bent over from many years of lifting people out of the gutters. Her face was deeply wrinkled, and her large, knotted hands looked battered from the years of cleaning toilets and wounds of the dying.

Yet Mother Teresa moved to the podium with the energy of a woman half her age. She spoke without notes, from her heart, her steel eyes glistening with a purpose. She begged mothers and fathers to spend time with their children, giving them love. She spoke of the smile on a dying man's face. The man, half eaten by worms, had been brought to Nirmal Hriday, where the sisters were caring for him. He said, "I have lived like an animal in the street, but I am going to die like an angel, loved and cared for." Mother Teresa called that man great because of the way he had died. She spoke of the many sacrifices people had made to help her work. And she asked each person who heard her words to re-member "that God loves me, and I have an opportunity to love others as He loved me, not in big things, but in small things with great love."

True to her own words, Mother Teresa used the Nobel Peace Prize money to start another home for lepers, where her sisters could, in small ways, serve the suffering.

Chapter 9

The Work Continues

Despite her advancing age and a heart condition that caused her great pain, Mother Teresa continued her work in Calcutta and in countries all over the world. Each time she would leave the Mother House, her sisters would gather around, giving her words of encouragement and asking her to return soon.

Mother Teresa has devoted more than forty years of her life to helping needy people around the globe.

Whenever Mother Teresa was due to arrive at one of her other houses, there would be great excitement. Then, when she did arrive, the cry "Mother is here!" would spread throughout the house.

Delivering a Message of Love

Mother Teresa, with her ready smile and ability to make each person feel special, continued to deliver her message of love wherever she felt it was needed.

Mother Teresa visits with children in Northern Ireland, where the Catholics are at war with the Protestants.

• In Northern Ireland, there was a war going on between Protestants and Catholics. Mother Teresa, herself a Catholic, flew to Northern Ireland to ask Protestant leader Ian Paisley how the war could be stopped.

• In the midst of another war, this time in Israel, Yasir Arafat, leader of the Palestine Liberation Organization, called on Mother Teresa, and she asked him to work for peace.

• In Beirut, Lebanon, another war was raging. But Mother Teresa had heard that there were 37 children in the city who needed help. The children, many of them retarded and desperately ill, were in a hospital that had been bombed, and no one could get medical supplies to them. Mother Teresa flew to Beirut to rescue the children. She was told that was impossible, that if she attempted to cross the city she would be killed in the crossfire. She said she would go the next day, when the

Mother Teresa at a Missionaries of Charity school in East Beirut, Lebanon.

Former mayor of New York, Ed Koch, met with Mother Teresa to discuss helping AIDS patients.

fighting stopped. People looked at her as if she was crazy; the fighting hadn't stopped in months! It didn't stop at that moment either. It continued through the night and into the next day, until the time came when Mother Teresa had said there would be a cease-fire. At that moment, as if by magic, the fighting stopped. An ambulance carrying the tiny nun raced across the silent city. Mother Teresa whisked the children away and brought them to safety. Only then did the fighting begin once more.

• In New York City, Mayor Edward Koch had been unable to get funding to help victims of AIDS. The Mayor remembered that Mother Teresa had visited him

not long before to say she wanted to open
a hospital for babies with AIDS. Koch
called Mother Teresa and told her that it
was adult AIDS victims who needed her
help most. The Gift of Love Home for
adult AIDS victims, run by the Missionaries
of Charity, opened within weeks.

• In California, a man had been
condemned to death because he had com-
mitted a murder. Mother Teresa picked up
the phone in India and called the governor of California to plead for the man's
life. She knew the man was guilty, but she
did not believe in capital punishment.

It seemed that Mother Teresa, just one
person living a life of poverty in India, was
everywhere. In a 1987 *Ladies Home Journal*
poll, Mother Teresa was named one of the
ten most important women in the world.

As always, Mother Teresa's response was,
"I am nothing. God is all."

Mother Teresa continued to work at the
same pace she had all her life despite doc-
tor's warnings that her heart could not
stand the strain. Even after a severe heart
attack in 1989, Mother Teresa continued to
work. One newspaper reported that same
year that she had been taken away again by
ambulance. But the next day, the newspaper said that the report had been wrong.

Mother Teresa had seen an accident and had rushed to help the victims so quickly that reporters thought it was Mother Teresa who had been hurt.

But Mother Teresa was weakening. In December of 1989, doctors put a device called a pacemaker in her heart to control its beating. Mother Teresa stopped traveling and worked only in her home city, Calcutta. Then, even that work became too much. Quietly, in the spring of 1990, she announced that she would be retiring as the head of the Missionaries of Charity. But, in September, she decided not to retire despite her poor health.

Mother Teresa's work had begun when she stepped outside the gates of her convent, alone, to work for the poor in the *bustees* of Calcutta. But 40 years later, at age 79, more than 3,000 sisters, 500 brothers, a new order of priests, and millions of Co-Workers were laboring for the Missionaries of Charity in 87 countries.

Most people would say Mother Teresa has been a success. But to Mother Teresa, numbers never mattered. "I do not add up. I only subtract from the total dying," she once said.

No one knows who will take Mother Teresa's place. Sister Agnes, the first

The Sisters of Charity pray for Mother Teresa's recovery after her heart attack in 1989.

young woman who had joined Mother Teresa in the work more than 40 years earlier, was 60 years old and too ill herself to run the order. Mother Teresa is not worried, however. As she has done all her life, she will patiently wait to see what God's plan will be. "We will act the way He leads us," she says.

Mother Teresa had once called herself "a little pencil" in the hand of God. She explained, "He does the thinking. He does the writing. The pencil has nothing to do with it. The pencil has only to be allowed to be used."

Mother Teresa would say that she had allowed God to use her in service to the poor for 40 years. Mother Teresa has no doubt that God will find another "little pencil" willing to be used to write His story.

Glossary

Explaining New Words

atheist A person who does not believe in God.

bustee A small village or slum in India.

caste A class of people in Hindu society. People are expected to stay in the caste into which they were born.

cease-fire The temporary stopping of fighting during a war.

charity The giving of time or money to the poor, ill, and helpless.

chastity The state of being chaste, or remaining a virgin.

cholera A highly contagious disease found mainly in India and China.

contagious Tending to spread easily from person to person.

dispensary A place where medicines are given out.

famine An extreme shortage of food leading to mass starvation.

Hindu A person who practices Hinduism, a religion based in India.

leper A person who has the disease leprosy. In India, a leper is also called an untouchable or outcast.

leprosy A disease that spreads easily in very warm climates and that affects the nervous system and skin.

maggot The soft-bodied, legless larvae of certain flies.

mass A service of the Catholic church.

Muslim A person of the Islam faith.

rupėe A coin used in India.

sacrifice To give up something important for the sake of someone else.

sari A garment worn by Hindu women. A sari is made of a long piece of cloth that is wrapped around the body.

For Further Reading

Craig, Mary. *Mother Teresa.* London: Hamish Children's Books, 1983.

Giff, Patricia Riley. *Mother Teresa: Sister to the Poor.* New York: Viking Kestrel, 1986.

Greene, Carol. *Mother Teresa: Friend of the Friendless.* Chicago: Children's Press, 1983.

Sebba, Anne. *Mother Teresa.* London: Julia MacRae Books, 1982.

Teresa, Mother, with Gonzalez-Balado, José Luis and Playfoot, Janet, eds. *My Life for the Poor.* San Francisco: Harper & Row, 1985.

Index

A

Agnes, Sister, 23, 58-59
Agra, India, 43-44
AIDS, 56
Andrew, Brother, 42
Arafat, Yasir, 54

B

Beirut, Lebanon, 55-56
Bengal, India, 17
Bible, 27
Blaikie, Ann, 39, 45-46
Bojaxhiu, Agnes Gonxha, 11
Brothers of Charity, 43
Brown, Jerry, 49
Bustees, 13, 58

C

Calcutta, India, 6, 12, 16-21
California, 57
Caste system, 20, 31
Children, 34-35, 43-44
Co-Workers of Mother Teresa,
    39-40, 45, 58
Cows, 20

D

Darjeeling, India, 12, 14
Das, Subashini, 23

Day of Inspiration, 14
Death, 35-37
Dispensaries, 41

E

East Pakistan, 17

G

Gandhi, Indira, 46
Gift of Love Home, 57
Gomes, Michael, 22, 38

H

Henry, Father, 22, 38-39
Hindus, 8-9, 10, 20, 33, 39
Holy Hour, 26

I

India, 12, 17, 31
Ireland, 12, 54
Israel, 54

J

Jacobsen, Mark, 48-49

K

Koch, Edward, 56

L

Ladies Home Journal, 57
Lepers, 30-32, 40-41, 43, 45
Leprosy, 30-32

M

Mary (mother of Jesus), 12
Missionaries, 12
Missionaries of Charity
  daily life of, 25-28
  God and, 11, 12, 14, 27-28,
    32, 49, 59
  help by, 15, 26-28, 30, 31, 35,
    36, 42, 44
  homes of, 30, 38-39, 42, 44,
    47, 57
  members of, 24-25, 42-43, 58
  money and, 16, 3-34, 43-46,
    52
  travels of, 42, 46-47, 50, 54-57
Mother House, 38, 44, 47, 53
Moti Jhil, 13
Muslims, 33, 39

N

New York City, 56
Nirmal Hriday, 8-10, 27, 35-37,
  38, 49, 52
Nobel Prize, 5, 47, 50-52
Northern Ireland, 54
Nuns, 8-9, 12, 15, 24-25

P

Paisley, Ian, 54
Patna, India, 15
Pope, The, 15, 38, 44

S

Sacrifice, 32-34
St. Mary's High School, 13, 14,
  23
Shantinagar, 30, 31-32
Sisters of Charity, 25, 34, 43
Sisters of Loreto, 12, 13, 14
Skopje, Yugoslavia, 11, 12
Sodality of Mary, 11
South America, 47

T

Teresa, Mother
  awards of, 5, 44, 47, 50-52
  childhood of, 11
  convent and, 12, 15-17, 38
  diary of, 21
  health of, 27, 53, 57, 58
  medical training of, 15
  name of, 11, 12-13, 15
  as teacher, 12, 13, 14, 22
Teresa, Saint, 13
Tower, Courtney, 48

U

Untouchables, 31, 41

Photo credits:

Cover, p.1: Gamma-Liaison/Santosh Basak; p.4: Dilip Mehta/Contact Stock; pps. 6,18:
The Bettmann Archive; pps. 7,23,29,30,31,32,37,48,50,51,53,54,55,56: AP/Wide World
Photos; p. 8: Religious News Service; pps. 11,13,16: SPCK; p.12: Eastfoto; p.19,45,49:
UPI/Bettmann Newsphotos; p.35: Gamma-Liaison/J.C. Francolon; p.26:Mary Ellen
Mark/Library; p.38: Catholic News Service; p.42: Chris Sheridan/Catholic News Service;
p.59: Reuters/Bettmann Newsphotos; p.60: Susan Meiselas/Magnum Photos.